Manchester
Then and Now
Text by Peter Riley

P & D Riley

First published 2003

P & D Riley
12 Bridgeway East
Cheshire WA7 6LD
England

E-mail: pdriley@ntlworld.com

ISBN:1 874712 61 1

British Library Cataloguing in Publication Data
A catalogue record for this book is available from the British Library
of the publisher and the copyright owner.

Printed in England.

Introduction

Manchester is a city that constantly evolves. Ever since the Romans first set up a base at Castlefields, just off today's Deansgate, the area has been on the move. The Romans called the place Mancunium, and built the first roads, but there is evidence that Manchester as a settlement existed even before then, with stone, flint and bronze weapons being found at various stages in its history.

Early Manchester was a sensible staging post for excursions in the wild reaches of northern Lancashire, especially from a defensive point of view, for to the south was the Mersey valley, then a huge marsh that was prone to flooding, while to the east stood the mighty Pennines, and to the north the hills and waters of the Lake District.

Manchester remained a small town for centuries, being described in 1724 as the "largest, most rich, populous and busy village in England," despite only having 2,300 families in the entire parish! In 1821 the population had risen to 187,031 and it was not until the Industrial Revolution that hundreds of thousands of people moved from the countryside into urban living, and by 1915 it boasted 738,538 people within its boundaries and was known the world over as 'Cottonopolis' being, as it then was, the heart of the British cotton industry with threads also stretching out to all parts of the British Empire thanks to the Manchester Ship Canal.

Today much of Manchester's industrial might has disappeared, and has been replaced with travel, computer technology and a thousand and one other business enterprises that our forefathers could not even dream about. Because of the changes in the city over the past century or so, it is fascinating to compare how the city's appearance has altered beyond recognition in some cases, yet in other cases has remained almost the same.

The majority of the older photographs in this book show Manchester as it was when cotton was king, and we have attempted to show comparison pictures as the same spots look today. In some cases, because of modern developments, we have not been able to photograph from the exact location of the original photographers, but we have done our best and hope the end results prove worthwhile.

Peter Riley

Peter Riley is the author and editor of numerous local history titles, including *Wythenshawe A Bygone Era (with Susan Hall)*; *Wythenshawe Hall and the Tatton family*; *Heaton Hall and the Egerton Family*; *A History of Peel Hall (with Susan Hall)*; *A Short History of Culcheth (with Oscar Plant)*; *The Highways and Byways of Jack the Ripper*; *Place to Place*; *Stockton Heath A Bygone Era*; *Culcheth A Bygone Era*; *Lowton A Bygone Era*; *Knutsford A Bygone Era*; *Bury A Bygone Era*; *Leigh, Tyldesley and Atherton A Bygone Era*; *Newton-le-Willows A Bygone Era*; *Hyde A Bygone Era*; *Newton-le-Willows in Bygone Days*; *A History of Leigh*; *A History of Atherton*; *A History of Tyldesley*; *A History of Astley*; *A History of Bolton*; *A History of Widnes*; *A History of Flixton*; *Then and Now (Leigh)*; *Warrington Then and Now.*

Acknowledgements

The publisher would like to thank the following for their help during the
preparation of this book

The Local Studies Library at
Manchester Central Library

Christopher D. Bathurst of Messrs Christopher/Dee
of Cross Street, Manchester

Messrs Carillion, site agents for No 1 Piccadilly, for allowing access to their
construction site

Elaine Chadwick and staff at Top Shop,
Arndale Centre, Manchester for their co-operation

Mosley Street: Queen Victoria was still on the throne and all was well on the home front when this photograph of Mosley Street and Princess Street was taken about 1896. The horse drawn bus at the front was on its way to Old Trafford from Piccadilly, and Mosley Street was busy with office workers and shoppers. The new Manchester Art Gallery is pictured on the right of the picture, and this photograph shows some of the other fine buildings that once stood on this street but have since been replaced with more functional but less impressive properties.

London Road Railway Station: Another photograph taken about 1896 showing the Victorian might and splendour of what was then called London Road Railway Station and now known simply as Piccadilly Station. This landmark only disappeared in the late 1950s to be replaced by the present glass and concrete structure and a sweeping facade of shops that replaced the old warehouses on the left. In the mid Victorian era a price war between companies using the station saw passengers being offered train journeys to London for as low as five shillings (25p).

Piccadilly Gardens 1935: For generations of Mancunians Piccadilly Gardens in the city centre was the heart of Manchester and a place of refuge and relaxation during summer months. The gardens had been created after the demolition of the old Manchester Infirmary at the turn of the 20th century, and the former basement made a fine sunken garden, complete with attractive flower beds. Following the removal of the nearby bus station to the Arndale Centre the gardens deteriorated, with renovations below making the gardens completely unrecognisable from their glory days.

Royal Exchange, 1896: What a magnificent building the Royal Exchange in Cross Street was in its Victorian heyday. It is still one of Manchester's most inspiring buildings, but its touch of class seemed to disappear when city planners approved the complete alteration to its portico façade in 1915. Despite the First World War Manchester's importance as the country's cotton centre was paramount, and the Exchange pictured above was considered too small to accommodate the hundreds of businessmen who flocked to the city on market days.

Town Hall and Albert Square, 1896 Anyone visiting Manchester can hardly fail to be impressed with its Town Hall. Opened in 1877 at a cost of around one million pounds, this centre of civic pride reflected the vast wealth and importance of Manchester in the 19th and early 20th centuries. To the right of the picture is the Albert Memorial, erected by public subscriptions in memory of Queen Victoria's late Prince Consort. The square, pictured below as it looks today, is still a vital part of today's city, with coffee bars and restaurants on the periphery. Behind the memorial is the Town Hall extension.

Deansgate, 1896: Looking at Deansgate above in the last decade of the 19th century, and below as it looks today, it is difficult to imagine that only 20 years before the top picture was taken Deansgate was known for its low criminal dens and appalling poverty. Manchester detective Jerome Caminada in his memoirs wrote: "Deansgate was a noted place for prize-fighting. In several of the beerhouse garrets there were regular rings...and many of the beerhouses (were) fitted up for dog-fights and 'drawing the badger'." Today Deansgate is one of the city's busiest and most affluent streets.

Exchange Station, 1896: Oliver Cromwell's statue stood guard outside Exchange Station for almost a century when road widening at this junction led to him being removed to the grounds of Wythenshawe Park six miles south of the city. This station, which opened in 1884 and closed in the 1960s, was one of Manchester's major railway stations, and once shared a platform with nearby Victoria Station, making it one of the longest in the world. Trains ran from Exchange to north of Manchester, though there was also a connection to London. Today nothing remains of the old station and its front approach is now a car park.

King Street, 1896: The building to the left of the photograph above shows the former Manchester Town Hall. When this building was demolished in the early 20th century the façade was dismantled and removed to Heaton Park, three miles north of the city, where it remains to this day overlooking the park's boating lake. King Street was (and remains) the centre of the city's banking and insurance institutions, and though changes have been made, the street retains an affluent air. The former offices of the Manchester Ship Canal Company were also once situated in this street.

Old Exchange Corner (St Ann's): Originally called Acresfield, this area of Manchester is now better known as St Ann's Square. Prior to 1788 when changes were afoot to improve this area of the city, the approach from the Exchange and Market Place to the square was described as mean and bad. Pedestrians made their way through a narrow passage which was so dismal and dark even during the middle of the day that it was known as the 'Dark Entry'. In 1776 an Act of Parliament was obtained to make changes, and a new street was built called Exchange Street. It remains unchanged to this day and is still a busy thoroughfare.

Portland Street: When the above photograph was taken about a century ago, Portland Street was lined with massive warehouses and offices to cope with the enormous amount of business generated through the cotton industry. Many of these buildings were still going strong for the selling of textiles until well into the 1970s, but with the industry declining many of the warehouses were demolished while others were converted to other uses. The photographs are looking towards Piccadilly, and it's hard to imagine this was once a lovely country area known as Garratt Lane!

Victoria Street and Deansgate: Even in 1896 when the photograph above was taken this part of Manchester was a busy place, with Victoria Street to the left full of horse drawn vehicles, heading to and from the Market Street area. We can see the old tower of the Royal Exchange in the distance. In Deansgate on the right we can see horse drawn omnibuses plying their trade along one of the city's major thoroughfares. Compare the traffic then with how the same scene looks today as pictured below.

The Town Hall Extension: After the Central Library in St Peter's Square was built in 1934, work began on building the Town Hall Extension next door. Designed by Vincent Harris it was to be eight storeys high with a unique 200 foot wall that was curved to parallel the shape of the library, and it was reckoned by many experts to be his best work. The building also includes a large council chamber on the first floor level. Total cost of the building was £750,000 and it was opened officially by King George VI in 1938. It is also home to the city's Tourist Information Office.

Piccadilly in 1896: A fascinating photograph of Piccadilly taken in the 1890s shows that this part of the city was a hive of activity even then. The massive building on the right was the old Manchester Infirmary that was eventually demolished, allowing an open space known as Piccadilly Gardens. Despite the many changes that have taken place here in recent years, visitors from the Victorian age would probably be able to recognise this scene if they could return today.

York Street, 1896: This was another Manchester street that was heavily dependent on the cotton industry and the grandeur of many of its buildings at the time the above photograph was taken reflects this. York Street was (and is) a tiny street situated between Portland Street and Fountain Street, and connected, therefore, the industrial might of the city with the banking centre of Manchester . Many banks still have their offices in this part of the city, but this area is now better know for its Chinese businesses and is on the fringe of Manchester's Chinatown.

Manchester Airport: No one visiting Manchester Airport today would be able to believe the changes that have taken place at Ringway since the above photograph was taken in 1949. The airport was then merely a small cluster of buildings that had just gone into the commercial sector after being an important training base for upto 600,000 troops of Britain's Airborne forces during the Second World War. In the 1950s and 60s its expansion really began, with massive growth in the 1970s, 80s and 90s, making it one of the country's main gateways to Europe and the world.

Manchester Art Gallery: A ubiquitous policeman stands directing traffic at the corner of Mosley Street and Princess Street in the above photograph taken about a century ago, with the Manchester Art Gallery behind him. This scene has changed very little in 100 years, with the exception of the large amount of traffic that now passes this corner. The building on the extreme left has long ago disappeared to be replaced by a monotonous looking office block. The art gallery, which was designed by Sir Charles Barry who later designed the Houses of Parliament, has recently benefited from a £35m transformation.

Old Wellington Inn, 1949: This ancient public house must be one of the most moved structures anywhere in the world! Situated in the old Market Place in the city centre, the entire surroundings of the Wellington Inn were destroyed in wartime bombing in 1940-41 and it seemed as though the pub was indestructible. However, in the 1960s new planning of the city meant the entire structure was raised several feet and moved to a new site. Another bomb, this time in 1996 by IRA terrorists, again saw the surrounding area devastated, and again the inn survived. Reconstruction once more followed, and the inn was moved again to its present site.

Oxford Street and the Palace Theatre:

The Palace Theatre on the right was known as the 'Palace of Dreams' for the many extravagant shows and top acts it attracted from around the world. Oxford Street was also a street of dreams for it was home to many of the city's top cinemas and music halls. Just past the Palace is St James's Buildings, once known as St James's Hall. Concerts were held here every week and were known as a 'Saturday Popular'. Today (below) it is home to offices of many of Manchester's major companies

Piccadilly Gardens: The photograph above was taken in 1949 and is interesting because it shows the city centre location known to every Mancunian in its transition from the austerity days of the Second World War to a city starting to move forward towards a new decade. Traffic was beginning to build up, though Manchester still had few private cars, and still boasted of having a fair share of horse drawn traffic, an example of which is seen in the bottom right hand corner. The scene below shows the same spot as it looks today.

Wythenshawe Park: In 1935 (above) the people of Manchester travelled to Wythenshawe Park to enjoy a day out away from the smoke and grime of the city. The park had only become public property in 1926 after Lord and Lady Simon, who had bought it off the historic Tatton family, donated it to Manchester for use as a public park. Wythenshawe Hall, the former Tudor home of the Tatton's, is pictured in the background. The wing on the left was later demolished. The hall is pictured below as it now looks.

District Bank, Spring Gardens: Massively proportioned buildings were the order of the day in the centre of Manchester in the Victorian era, as the 1896 photograph above shows. Spring Gardens, however, was once a place of beauty, and in the early 19th century a few houses stood in this area, but open fields extended to the gardens on the south side. In one of the gardens a spring supplying clean, pure water had been discovered and this source was seen as vital to those living here. It gave the district the name by which it is still known and saw the area grow and prosper until it became the very heart of Manchester's financial district.

Oxford Road: One of the main arteries into the city centre from the south, Oxford Road is also home to Manchester Museum and the University and the headquarters of the BBC. Until recent years it was also a road which boasted some of the area's most interesting buildings, many of them in close proximity to each other, but these have mainly disappeared though development. Oxford Road is, however, still proud of the former Refuge Assurance Building, now a hotel, and the Church of the Holy Name which was built by Joseph Hansom, better known to historians as the inventor of the famous Hansom cab.

Albert Square: This square, named in honour of Prince Albert whose memorial we can see in the centre of both photographs, although taken a century apart, is one of the city's main meeting points, with Christmas concerts held here, and homecomings for many of sporting heroes of Manchester. The citizens of Manchester paid for the memorial which cost £6,249 without the statue. It was once described as one of the world's most ugly objects, though this was definitely an exaggeration, for in today's plastic and glass society, the ornate carving of the statue and memorial is its greatest asset, giving a touch of class to this lovely square.

Market Place: Yet another photograph taken in 1896 of the old Market Place. Sadly this fascinating jumble of buildings was destroyed during the bombing of Manchester in the Second World War. This was once one of the city's busiest areas, and it is interesting that 'Ye Olde Fishing Tackle Shoppe' should be so prominent (top picture) in a city centre. The city has two rivers close by, the Irk and the Irwell, but when the above picture was taken they were so polluted no fish could survive! The area has since been extensively redeveloped as we can see from the picture below.

Manchester University: The university today has more than 18,000 full-time students, including 2,500 international students, from over 120 countries, and is a far cry from its humbler beginnings as Owens College in Quay Street, Manchester, in the mid-19th century. The foundation stone was laid by the Duke of Devonshire, president of the fund-raising committee, in September 1870. The complex also houses the recently extended and improved Manchester Museum.

Near St Peter's Square, Oxford Street. One of the main thoroughfares in and out of the city, Oxford Street has always been busy with trams and buses carrying passengers to the south of Manchester, particularly to Fallowfield, Withington, Didsbury and Chorlton. This part of the street was also home to many theatres (later cinemas) and music halls. In recent years many of the old buildings and former theatres, including the old Princes Theatre on the right, have been torn down and replaced with office blocks and restaurants.

Portland Street and Princess Street: Another fascinating photograph showing one of the busiest junctions in Manchester. We are looking up Portland Street towards Piccadilly and on the right, halfway up, we can get a clear idea of the size of the former S & J Watts warehouse that once dominated this part of the street. Many of the older buildings on the street have since disappeared, and pedestrians would be taking their lives in their hands if they crossed this junction so casually today. The open topped tram appears to be on its way to Exchange Station, probably travelling via Oxford Street, Peter Street and Deansgate.

Mosley Street and Princess Street corner:

This wonderful photograph says it all about how busy Manchester was in the early 20th century, with the tram, hansom cab on the left and an early motor vehicle on the right. The policeman standing in the middle of the road appears to be totally in charge of proceedings on this busy spot outside the city's Art Gallery.

St Mary's Gate: The appearance of a photographer always attracted attention in the streets of Manchester as can be witnessed by the curious looks from youngsters and adults alike as this cameraman snapped this busy scene in old Manchester, close to Deansgate. The fine buildings in this area have now disappeared but the street, situated between Deansgate and Corporation Street, remains. It appears that this has always been one of the busiest areas of Manchester, and remains so to this day, though sadly lacking its previous character.

Market St, near Lewis's: What an elaborate frontage the old Lewis's store had when this photograph was taken in the 1890s, with fancy lamp-standards to make the corner stand out from across Piccadilly and down Market Street. Alas Lewis's, one of Manchester's most famous and favourite stores for a century, is no more! Market Street has always been one of the city's busiest streets and as long ago as the turn of the 20th century there was talk of it becoming pedestrianised, though this idea was not achieved until the 1970s. Where the horse drawn cart once stood now stands a staging post for the new Metro-Link tram system.

Deansgate 1890s: A fine atmospheric photograph of Manchester's famous thoroughfare, complete with plenty of horse-drawn traffic and given wonderful depth thanks to the photographer including the decorative gap lamp on the left of the picture. The Deansgate area of the city was becoming busy with shops and offices and the sign on the top right hand side, saying simply "Persia, China, Japan' suggests a shipping agent worked here, probably sending cotton goods made in and around Manchester to these 'foreign' parts. Goods from here were also sent to all parts of the British Empire, then at its zenith.

Piccadilly corner: This must be one of the most famous sights of Manchester, for anyone who has strolled from Piccadilly Station along London Road will have been confronted with this scene of Piccadilly looking towards Market Street in the distance. It is hard to believe that this part of Manchester was once known as Daub Holes and was out in the country, beyond the city boundaries. To the right of the photograph is Lever Street, named after the Lever family who once had a mansion called Lever's Hall close by.

Smithfield Market: It is heartening to know that the facade of the old Smithfield Market hall on the left is still standing, though the rest of the buildings in the above picture have long since been demolished. Until the 1960s and early 70s this was one of the busiest and most bustling parts of the city, with the streets packed with carts, lorries and vehicles of every description, bringing produce to Manchester from all parts of Britain. It was particularly busy from 5am until about 10am. The old market closed when a more modern one was built two miles away in Openshaw.

Clayton Hall: This ancient hall just two miles from the city centre was once the home of one of the city's most influential men, Sir Humphrey Chetham. Reached by a stone bridge that crosses a now dry moat, the house, with its green lawns, was once regarded as a gem in this part of East Manchester . Dating from about the 16th century it has been extensively renovated over the years, though it remains one of the few rural bright spots in this part of an otherwise run down area of the city. It was here that Chetham, who gave Manchester a magnificent library, died in 1653.

Town Hall:

The dramatic impact of Manchester Town Hall can never be underestimated. It is a magnificent building, though for the best part of the 20th century the building looked far from its best for it was so coated with smoke and soot from the tens of thousands of coal fires in the city that it was totally black. In 1977 to commemorate its 100th birthday, it was given a thorough sandblasting that brought back its superb warm colour, and it remains one of the real jewels in Manchester's crown.

The Town Hall is shown above as it looked in about 1900, while the bottom photograph shows how the same scene looks today.

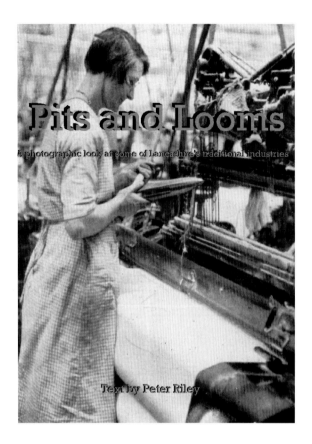